DL 66

You Be the Judge

Lessons to Build Evaluative Thinking Skills

Judicial Decisions

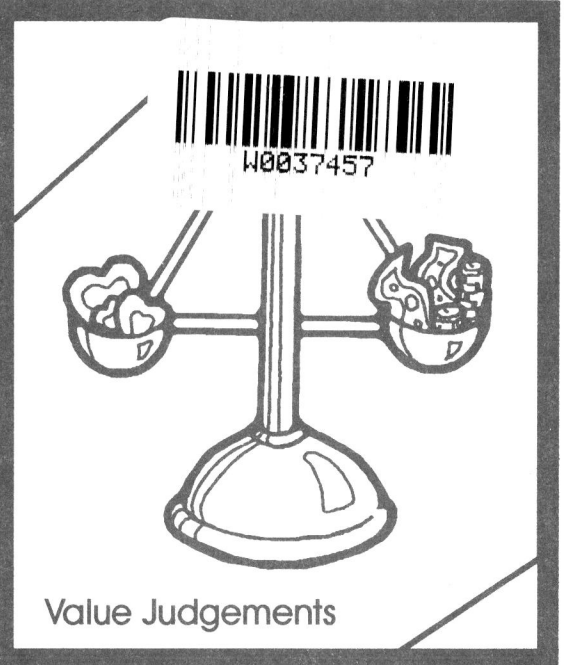

Value Judgements

Criteria Evaluations

Written by Barbara Juskow

Illustrated by Annelise Palouda

Edited by **Dianne Draze**

ISBN 0–931724–83–X

Contents

Introduction

Throughout our lives we are faced with situations that require decisions. Sometimes the decision is easy, and sometimes we have to wrestle with hard choices. It may be as simple as knowing that you love red and hate purple and, therefore, will buy the red sweater. More commonly, however, these decision situations require complex thought processes involving weighing many factors before making a final evaluation. By being aware of different techniques that can be employed to make decisions, we increase the likelihood of making rational decisions we can be happy with rather than jumping to intuitive decisions that we soon regret.

It is important, therefore, that children understand some of the methods people use to reach conclusions. A study of evaluation techniques not only gives students a chance to explore their own decision-making processes but also gives them a chance to understand how other people may come to opposite or different conclusions.

You Be the Judge explores three types of decision-making. They are criteria evaluation, value judgements and judicial decisions.

1. **Criteria Evaluation** - The first type of decision-making method is one that typically uses numbers. Some examples of situations that use this kind of judgement are figure skating, diving, gymnastics and report cards. In lessons that deal with this type of judgement, students will learn that the marks awarded in these situations are based on strict criteria. Students will also learn how to examine and develop their own criteria.

2. **Value Judgements** - The second decision-making situations are ones that call upon moral training and values learned at home, school and church. Students examine scenarios that cover situations ranging from mere personal preferences to serious dilemmas that have no right or good answers. This section of work is important for gaining insights and understanding into how others make decisions and helps students to explore their own values and reasoning processes.

3. **Judicial Decisions** - The third type of judgement situations puts the student in the role of an impartial observer in the disputes of other people. These situations require students to sift through and weigh the facts before making a decision. Through role-playing, students learn the importance of presenting the facts in a convincing manner. They also learn that judgements are often based on laws influenced by decisions made for similar situations in the past. Early beginnings of the law are explored briefly in this section.

In all of the lessons in this book students learn about decision-making by being involved in the processes of decision-making. They will be asked to become active participants — to weigh, to consider, to debate, and to cast judgements. Skills in these lessons include:

Fluency	Analysis
Flexibility	Synthesis
Originality	Evaluation
Elaboration	Risk Taking
Drama	Acceptance of others' ideas

You Be The Judge is organized in three sections — one for each evaluation technique. For each of the three sections you will find complete lesson plans for the instructor and reproducible worksheets for students.

Lessons for Criteria Evaluation

Lesson 1

Objective: Students will be able to identify the three types of evaluations that will be studied and give an example from their own lives of each type.

Accompanying Worksheet: Three Types of Evaluation, pages 16-17

Procedure:

1. This lesson is meant to be an overview of the whole course. Begin with a discussion of how students make decisions. Use the following scenarios or ones like them.

   a. How do you decide whether to buy a T-shirt for $14.99 or the blue dress shirt for $24.99?

   b. Suppose on your way home today you come across two bigger students pushing a smaller student around. The bullies are bigger than you. What's the right thing for you to do? The best thing? How does the decision you make affect you? How does it affect the person being bullied?

   c. Two of your friends have had a serious argument. Each of them has come to you separately and asked you to help settle the dispute. What are the logical steps you should take to restore your group to friendship again.

2. Introduce the three different types of evaluations — criteria evaluation, value judgements, and judicial decisions. Pass out the worksheet. Discuss each evaluation technique.

3. During the discussion, make a wall chart that has a space for each technique and make note of sample situations that would call for each judgement technique and a few key words to identify the technique. Later as each type of evaluation is studied, students can refer to the charts to see how the solutions to everyday problems fit each category. It's also a good idea to record some of the personal scenarios students will tell about during the discussion. These scenarios can be used later during the lessons for each technique.

4. Reinforce the idea that people solve problems and make decisions by using several different methods and that by learning different ways of thinking about choices and courses of action they will be able to make better decisions.

Journals:

This program lends itself well to journal writing. Because personal feelings and moral issues are discussed, sometimes students have opinions they may not wish to share with the group, but ones they would be willing to record in a journal. If you choose to have students write journals, pass out or assemble notebooks at this time.

Worksheet Answers

1. VJ	2. CE
3. CE	4. JD
5. VJ	6. JD
7. VJ	8. CE

Lesson 2

Objective: Students will be able to choose the most important criteria from a list of criteria.

Accompanying Worksheet: Considering Criteria, page 18

Procedure:

1. Give the definition of criteria as rules or standards people use to judge things. Talk about criteria you have when you grade a student's creative writing assignment (story development, characterization, vocabulary, spelling, capitalization, use of complete sentences) or criteria a student might use when deciding which way to get home (distance, which way a friend is going, whether there are vicious dogs on the way, whether there are errands to do that would require a particular route, weather, etc.). Discuss the fact that when making a decision, each individual might have different criteria. Therefore, people often arrive at different decisions when faced with the same choices. When we are making individual choices, it is usually okay to have different criteria from other people. If we are judging a competition (like a diving meet) it is important that all the judges have the same standards.

2. Hand out the worksheet. Have students select the three most important criteria for each situation.

3. Discuss other situations in which people use criteria to judge the value or merit of various alternatives. For each situation, suggest several possible criteria. If students have no suggestions, you could use the following situations:

- grading a math assignment
- deciding the winner of a poetry contest
- deciding which bike to buy
- deciding which new pet to get
- deciding the order in which to do homework.

Lesson 3

Objective: Students will be able to brainstorm possible solutions and select the best idea based on given criteria.

Accompanying Worksheet: Brainstorming Criteria, pages 19-21

Procedure:

1. Discuss the concept that by having several solutions to a problem, you increase your likelihood of making a good choice. Explain that if students only think of one possibility, this solution may or may not be the best. By thinking of several different possibilities, they have a better chance of making the best decision.

2. Choose one of the three situations. Have students work together in small groups of two or three to brainstorm ideas for the situation. You may want to have students fold their papers in such a way that they cannot see the criteria. In this way, they will not prejudge their ideas. Give students enough time to produce a sizeable list. Remind them to think of as many ideas as possible, to jot them down quickly, and to defer judgement of all ideas until later. Some goofy ideas may turn out to be great. If you wish to use an anecdote to convince them that deferring judgement can be valuable, tell them the following true story.

"A large oil company wanted to find ways to save money on their drilling operations. The company called its group of managers together to discuss the problem. It was discovered that one expense seemed excessive. Each time a drill was put into the ground, a small metal casing had to be used to protect the drill tip. The metal casing was ruined and impossible to retrieve as soon as drilling began. The team of managers was asked to find an alternate solution to the problem. After hours of brainstorming and evaluating each idea the company wound up using what might have been thought a "goofy" idea — paper. Pressed paper casings were tried and they worked. The company saved money. It's a good thing no one on the team said, "That won't work. You can't use paper to drill into rock."

3. After they have brainstormed a list of ideas, have them choose the five best ideas and write them on the evaluation chart. Have each student complete the evaluation chart independently of other group members.

The ideas each student chooses do not have to be the same as the ideas chosen by other members of their group. Explain that to weigh each idea they must have rules or criteria to apply and think about. Have students refer to the criteria. They should rate each idea against the first criteria, giving the idea that best meets the criteria a 5, the next best idea a 4, and so forth. The first criteria should be applied to each idea first, then the second idea, and so on. They should rate all ideas with each criteria before considering the next criteria.

4. Repeat with other two situations.

Lesson 4

Objective: Students will be able to list criteria for given decision situations.

Accompanying Worksheet: Making Rules to Evaluate Your Ideas, pages 22-23

Procedure:

1. Review how criteria are used to rate ideas. Discuss how two people making the same decision might have different criteria and, therefore, might make different decisions. An example might be two girls trying to decide on which dress to buy. One person might think style, color and price are important. Another girl might not care about color or price at all. Her criteria might be style, easy care, and warmth. They would probably choose different dresses.

2. Distribute worksheet. Have students list possible criteria for each situation. In the development of criteria students should be encouraged to talk about what is important and, if possible, to rank order the criteria. Are some criteria more important than others?

3. Discuss students' criteria. When there are differences of opinion, students should be given a chance to talk about them.

Lesson 5

Objective: Students will be able to evaluate candidates based on criteria they create.

Accompanying Worksheets: Choosing a Class President, pages 24-29

Procedure:

1. Begin the lesson by asking students to recall a time when they had to vote for another person in order to choose a leader or select someone for a job. How did they make the decision? Did they vote for a friend? Did they vote for the most popular person? How do they think their parents make their choices when they vote? Are they influenced by the opinions of others?

   Discuss the role of leadership. What kind of person do they wish to have represent them? What qualities do they think a group leader or school representative should have?
   Then discuss how ideal personality traits are exhibited by people running for office. Sometimes it is difficult to tell whether a person is honest, responsible and reliable when you don't know the person personally.

2. Hand out the first worksheet, (page 24). With a partner have students first brainstorm a list of personal qualities for a candidate and then a list of changes they would like a leader of their school to initiate.

3. Have students choose the three criteria for personal qualities and three for school improvements that they think are the most important. Record these on the evaluation sheet (page 29).

4. Pass out information on candidates (pages 25-28). Have students read through descriptions of each person either silently or by having a few students assume the roles of the candidates and read the speeches. Have

students rate each candidate on the evaluation chart (page 29) using their pre-selected criteria. Discuss choices and reasoning.

Lesson 6

Objective: Students will be able to rank criteria according to which ones they think are most important.

Accompanying Worksheet: Putting Your Criteria in Order, page 30

Procedure:

1. Hand out worksheet. Have students rank the qualities for a friend.

2. After students have completed the exercise there should be a discussion of what the group as a whole considers the five most important qualities and the three least important qualities. Give ample time for a full discussion of these.

3. Have students divide into partners and list three additional qualities.

Lesson 7

Objective: Students will be able to generate a list and then use given criteria to select the best item on the list.

Accompanying Worksheet: Play Time, page 31

Procedure:

1. Discuss the difference between work and play. Ask students to name some things they consider work and some they consider play.

2. Have students individually complete the worksheet by listing the things they consider fun leisure time activities and then use the given criteria to evaluate their five favorite activities.

3. A discussion should follow. Discuss personal preferences like why some people consider reading a book fun and some consider it boring.

Math Extension:

You might want to make a class graph of students' favorite activities.

Lesson 8

Objective: Students will be able to generate a set of criteria for evaluating items to purchase.

Accompanying Worksheet: Wish List, page 32

Procedure:

1. Discuss how everyone has a lot of things they want to buy but usually not enough money to buy everything. Discuss experiences students have had when they have made purchases they were later unhappy with. Why were they disappointed with these purchases?

2. Hand out the worksheet. Have students make wish lists. They should then list criteria for selecting items to buy and use criteria to evaluate five items on their list.

3. Share results of the evaluation. Discuss ways students could use a simplified process such as this to evaluate purchases they make on a daily basis.

Lesson 9

Objective: Students will be able to generate criteria for evaluating a learning experience, choose the most important criteria and use the criteria to judge a learning situation.

Accompanying Worksheet: Evaluating a Learning Experience, page 33

Procedure:

1. This is a summation of the lessons so far. Brainstorm together the criteria of a good learning experience. Some of the following may be suggested:

   - It was fun.
   - I learned something I didn't already know.
   - I wasn't frustrated.
   - I got a good feeling afterward.
   - I was praised during the lesson.
   - I felt my ideas were heard.
   - I could pass a test on the information.
   - I wasn't bored.
   - I got to talk about it instead of the teacher doing all the talking.

   Be open to suggestions of improvement. The more ownership the students feel they have in the material, the better the lesson will be.

2. Have students complete the worksheet by listing their criteria for a good learning experience and then using these criteria to evaluate each of their classes and choose the best class.

Lessons for Value Judgements

Lesson 10

Objective: Students will be able to rank situations to show their personal preferences in a variety of situations.

Accompanying Worksheet: Personal Preferences, pages 34-35

Procedure:

1. Review the definition of this type of evaluation (see page 16). Discuss how different backgrounds or different needs in society influence our decisions. A person's choices are often based upon past experiences. They choose the things they found they liked or the things that worked best for them in the past. In making up one's mind about what to choose or which course of action to take, people also apply the moral training they have been given at home, at church, and at school. Emotions, values and intuition are involved. Right behavior and overall goodness are considered. Sometimes no "right" answer can be reached and one is forced to choose the lesser of two "wrong" or "bad" choices. Decisions of this type are called dilemmas. Allow for a full discussion. The class should be reminded that in certain lines of work (police, the armed forces, and some government agencies) people are faced with dilemmas.

2. Complete the worksheet.

3. After doing the exercise allow time for discussion of any of the questions that students found particularly difficult or perhaps silly. Discuss how these personal preferences would lead people to make different choices.

Lesson 11

Objective: Students will be able to make a personal choice on a course of action for given situations in which personal values and standards for behavior are involved.

Accompanying Worksheet: Decisions! Decisions! page 36

Procedure:

1. Ask students to think about a time when it was hard for them to know what was the right thing to do. Share some examples. Discuss how some situations have no obvious right or wrong choice. Deciding what to do is based on what the individual feels is important.

2. Pass out and have students complete the worksheet.

3. After doing the worksheet and discussing the dilemmas, allow time for individuals to talk about any similar dilemmas they have experienced.

Follow-up:

The game of *Scruples for Children* fits well into this part of the program.

Lesson 12

Objective: Students will be able to decide between two conflicting choices based on their values.

Accompanying Worksheet: Decision Situations, page 37

Procedure:

1. Discuss the fact that getting something you want often means giving up something you have. Decisions are a commitment of personal resources — time, energy, money, relationships, goals, and self. Deciding is acting on our values. Our decision strategy includes an attempt to achieve or preserve either resources or values.

2. Hand out worksheet and have students work through the exercises.

3. Discuss students' decisions and why some students may make one decision while other students would choose something different. Both decisions may be "correct" depending on the values of the two individuals. Stress that often in dilemmas, students are faced with

having to give up one thing in order to get something else. By being aware of what they value most and what is at stake in these decision situations, it makes the decision clearer, if not easier.

Lesson 13

Objective: Students will be able to make a decision about a situation that involves personal morals and defend their decisions.

Accompanying Worksheet: Dilemma at the Birthday Party, page 38

Procedure:

1. Discuss the meaning of truth. Should you always tell the truth? Why or why not? Do you expect others to be truthful with you? Which people in your life do you trust the most to always be truthful with you? Explain that many dilemmas that young people face involve deciding whether to tell the truth or not. While each situation is slightly different, knowing your personal standards regarding truth-telling will help you make decisions you can be proud of.

2. Ask students to think about a time when they had to decide between being completely honest or telling a lie. Discuss briefly how they decided whether to tell the truth or not.

3. Pass out copies of the worksheet and have students read silently or read the story aloud to the class. After reading the story, ask each student to decide what they would do and explain why they would make that choice.

4. Discuss students' decisions and reasoning. Discuss the following questions:

   - Is anyone hurt if the older brother doesn't tell?
   - What is a conscience and why do we have one?
   - Should everyone at the party be punished if only a few of the guests went into the bedroom?

   You may also wish to discuss temptation and how giving in to temptations may spoil the thrill of anticipation that often heightens the final results (in this case, discovering what the special prizes are).

Lesson 14

Objective: Students will be able to make a decision about a situation that involves personal morals and defend their decisions.

Accompanying Worksheet: The Class Trip, page 39

Procedure:

1. This lesson may be used in addition to or instead of Lesson 13. Both lessons deal with having to make a decision to take an honest course of action or to give into peer pressure and tell a lie.

2. Pass out copies of the worksheet and have students read silently or read the story aloud to the class. After reading the story, ask each student to decide what they would do and explain why they would make that choice.

3. Discuss students' decisions and rationales. Discuss the following questions:
   - What should be done when a few break the rules and everyone has to pay?
   - What is peer pressure?
   - Who is hurt by the telling? By not telling?
   - How would students feel if they were one of the innocent parties? One of the ones who caused the trouble or broke the rules? One of the friends of a person who broke the rules?
   - If Marcela tells, what should the teacher do?
   - What obligations are we under when we are part of a group?

Lesson 15

Objective: Students will be able to make a decision that involves choosing between friends and family and explain their choices.

Accompanying Worksheet: The Promise, page 40

Procedure:

1. Begin with a discussion of the definition of a promise. What are some of the promises students have made in the past? What are some important promises? How does it feel when someone breaks a promise they made to you?

2. Pass out copies of the worksheet and have students read silently or read the story aloud to the class. After reading the story, ask each student to decide what they would do and explain why they would make that choice.

3. Discuss students' decisions and reasoning. Discuss promises that were made to them and broken. How did they feel about it? Why were they upset? Why do people break promises?

4. This dilemma involves how much a person values obligations to family versus obligations to friends. Discuss other situations that students have experienced that involve making a choice between family and friends. Why are these situations difficult?

Lesson 16

Objective: Students will be able to make a decision about a situation that involves personal morals and defend their decisions.

Accompanying Worksheet: The Garden, page 41

Procedure:

1. Ask students to think of tasks or chores they really dislike doing. Share some examples. Explain that they will be reading about a situation that involves an unpleasant task.

2. Pass out and read the worksheet. Have students respond to the questions.

3. The discussion after this lesson should center on the nature of dilemmas. There may be no right or good choice, or it could be that both choices are bad or wrong. In this case, if the person who makes the promise breaks the promise, he suffers a guilty conscience. A guilty conscience often damages a person's positive self-image. If the person who makes the promise keeps the promise, he is doomed to a lifetime of doing an unsavory task. This lesson can also lead to a discussion of learning to like something that you once didn't like.

4. Note that in this dilemma, there is no way to do nothing. In fact, doing nothing is doing something and is, therefore, a choice.

Lesson 17

Objective: Students will be able to make a decision involving giving possessions to friends and relatives.

Accompanying Worksheet: Share the Wealth, pages 42-43

Procedure:

1. Before this lesson discuss promises in the form of wills. By carrying out the terms of a will people are promising to keep a person's wishes after they die. Our society recognizes a legal responsibility to keep the promises made in wills.

2. Have students complete the exercises on the worksheet.

3. After students have written their wills, have them discuss on what basis they decided how to dispose of their possessions. Most students enjoy thinking about rewarding friends and relatives with their money and possessions. Generally, younger students will base their rewards on the recipient's need and worthiness. Every student should be given a chance to read his or her will aloud.

4. For an added dimension, have each student take the worksheet home and have family members make a joint decision on how to dispose of the possessions and then compare their will with the student's original will.

Lesson 18

Objective: Students will be able to make a decision involving obligations to one's group and defend their decisions.

Accompanying Worksheet: The New Planet Dilemma, page 44

Procedure:

1. Ask students to think about and share examples of decisions their parents, as the leaders of their families, must make. Discuss problems that might arise when one person (the leader) has to make decisions that affect the entire group. Point out that many of the decisions facing the head of a family are not complicated, but in other situations, leaders sometimes have to face situations where there are no simple choices.

2. Hand out and work through the worksheet.

3. Take a poll to find out how many would vote to put Smith out and how many would fight the natives. Discuss other alternatives for this dilemma. This lesson should focus on the problems of leadership. A good leader must do his or her best for the group. In the case of this dilemma, what is best? What's to stop the native chief from returning a week from now and demanding that Mary Jones be put out for torture because the natives believe she has magical powers that caused a failure of their cherry salt bubbles? Or conversely, should everyone be sacrificed by fighting to the death?

Lesson 19

Objective: Students will be able to analyze the various justifications for breaking rules and decide if it is right to break rules you don't agree with.

Accompanying Worksheet: Breaking the Rules, page 45

Procedure:

1. Is there excitement in, "getting away with something?" Discuss how students feel when they are torn between being called "chicken" and being looked down upon by their peers and following the rules and regulations because they know they have been established for their safety.

2. Have students read the story about breaking the rules on the worksheet and answer the questions.

3. Discuss how people decide whether to follow the rules or not. What problems might be caused if everyone only obeyed the rules they agreed with? If you don't hurt anyone else, is it okay to break rules?

Lessons for Judicial Decisions

Lesson 20

Objective: Students will be able to listen to two sides of a disagreement and decide which side presents the most believable arguments.

Accompanying Worksheet: Judge the Situation, pages 46-47

Procedure:

1. Begin with a discussion of the definition of judgement (see page 16) and relate judgement to the law. Weighing the facts is most important. Why is it best if an impartial person decides who is right and who is wrong? What qualities should a good judge have? Talk about who is judge at home when something goes wrong. Does a parent listen to both sides of the story? If a punishment is necessary, is the punishment based on past activities and punishments? Have any of the students ever had to play the role of judge in a dispute between friends? What's difficult about being a judge? How do you know if a person is telling you the truth when you are acting as a judge?

2. Hand out the list of predicaments on *Judge the Situation.* For each situation assign two actors. Actor's are to prepare their arguments. Judges listen carefully and list the points made by each actor. Then they must decide who gave the more positive, believable points to support his or her argument. You may choose to have the situations presented in such a way that the entire class must jointly decide what should be done.

3. Discuss what was important from the jury's point of view. What made one argument seem more believable than the other? Most court cases rely upon witness testimony. If the students were jurors what would they look for?

Lesson 21

Objective: Students will be able to make a list of rules for a new colony and analyze the rules in terms of their purpose.

Accompanying Worksheet: Making Rules, pages 48-49

Background Information:

You may wish to do a time line on the major developments that led to the present systems of law in North America.

10,000 B.C. - Cave dwellers - Governing rule was survival of the fittest.

1728 - 1686 B.C. - Code of Hammurabi -The first written laws and punishments were made by King Hammurabi of Babylon. By this time people had settled in communities and villages. There were too many laws to remember. Hammurabi revised the laws and had them inscribed into a column of granite where everyone had access to them. These laws were called edicts, laws made by the ruler. Hammurabi was the first to codify the laws. The 300 laws dealt with the same things our laws cover — sale and purchase, inheritance, marriage, theft and manslaughter.

1200 B.C. - Ten Commandments - Moses was considered a divinely chosen leader. He received the Ten Commandments from God. They defined principles of morality. During this time the laws improved in that they tried to make a difference between deliberate and accidental acts. They also tried to punish the guilty, not the innocent.

The Greeks promoted the idea that all Greek males were free and equal before the law. They developed the first jury system. They also developed the idea that rules should be changed when they ceased to meet the needs of the community.

451 B.C. - 180 B.C. - Roman Law - Law became more complex and individuals were trained to deal only with legal matters. These men were the first lawyers. Roman law was concerned mostly with the efficient administration of their territories. Much of modern law was influenced by Roman law.

1215 A.D. - The Magna Carta - King John affixed his seal to an agreement that allowed nobles to have some say in laws and punishments. This was the first step in taking some power away from the monarchy and guaranteeing civil rights. It became a model for citizens' rights.

1776 - Settlers in the new land, North America, developed our present systems of justice. These systems include a civil law component that is derived from the ideas of

Roman law and a common law component that is derived from early English Common Law. The Constitution of the United States was innovative in that it stated that legal authority was derived from its citizens, not from rulers. It has been a model for the constitutions of many other countries.

1804 A.D. - Napoleonic Code - Napoleon compiled the French code of law. It was based on existing French law and Roman law and was concerned with civil rather than criminal law. It became a strong influence for later legal systems. The province of Quebec still uses old Napoleonic laws.

Today, not only the government makes laws, but the judges also make laws by following the decisions of other judges and making new interpretations. We call these decisions precedents. Much of our law today is decided by a precedent.

Procedure:

1. Tell students that they will get a chance to make a new set of rules. Ask them to suggest some possible rules for their city or school. Discuss in a general sense why we have rules (to protect people's rights and property, to insure safety, to insure healthy living conditions, to enforce fairness and cooperation, to protect the environment, etc.).

2. Have students complete the worksheet. Students will do part of this worksheet on their own and part with a partner.

3. Compare rules, purposes of rules and punishments.

4. Save these rules. After you have finished the lessons in this section, you may want to go back and have students revise their rules. taking into consideration what they have learned.

Lesson 22

Objective: Students will be able to make judgements concerning historical cases and compare their judgements to judgements that were most likely issued under the ancient rules.

Accompanying Worksheet: Ancient Rules and Punishments, pages 50-51

Procedure:

1. Hand out copies of the worksheet. Have students read and judge each case.

2. Discuss as a group what the verdict should be.

3. Read the verdicts that were based on Hammurabi's laws. Students will be thoroughly horrified with the injustice of these verdicts. Explain that the King had total power and control. Little difference was made between an intentional deed and an accidental one. Often an accused man could buy his way free if he were wealthy enough. Ask students how they feel about Hammurabi's laws. Discuss what problems students see with Hammurabi's laws.

Answers

Case 1 - Errant Ox
Verdict based on Hammurabi's law: Thor was found guilty. Thor was a clever man and his popularity in the village was growing. The King distrusted him because he thought Thor might be a threat to his power.

Case 2 - Stolen Payment
Verdict based on Hammurabi's law: Both men were sentenced to death.

Case 3 - Child Abuse
Verdict based on Hammurabi's law: Kilgar's hands were cut off. The king's law said, "If a son has struck his father, his hands shall be cut off."

Case 4 - Drunken Behavior
Verdict based on Hammurabi's law: Poleth's daughter was put to death. Hammurabi's law clearly stated: If a man strikes a man's daughter and she dies, his own daughter shall be killed.

Lesson 23

Objective: Students will be able to write a law and then test it using several different cases.

Accompanying Worksheet: Design-a-Law, pages 52-54

Procedure:

1. Discuss how people must have felt during the reigns of kings like Hammurabi. From the time of Hammurabi to the time of the signing of the Magna Carta (3000 years) people knew no other form of law.

2. Have students brainstorm the qualities of a good law. List several qualities and then select the ones the students feel are most important. Generally a law is considered to be a good one if it has the following qualities. If necessary, subtly direct students so that their list of qualities includes these concepts.

   1. fair to most or all people
   2. clear and easy to follow
   3. easily understood
   4. punish the guilty and not the innocent
   5. not become outdated in the near future

3. Have each student write a law and then examine their law using the test cases. When doing the test cases discuss:

   Case 1 - Whether Mary Littlepink should be liable for the damages. Is this a special circumstance? Do their laws provide for such emergencies? Should the laws be reworded?

   Case 2 - If the students have included "for a good reason" in their laws in light of Mary Littlepink's predicament, challenge this with Bob Fingleprint's case. Bob feels he has a good reason — he planned to band this rare specimen, thus adding to the world's knowledge of how to preserve rare butterflies.

   Case 3 - Discuss Linda Lookalive's attitude. Does she have to follow a law made by someone she didn't vote for? A law she thinks is stupid? Did students include animals in their laws? Is Linda liable if the law does not clearly include animals?

   Case 4 - Is the boy who fell on the grass liable? Did the laws the students wrote say, "walk" or "on". If it said walk, would that include "run", "hop", "skip", etc.?

   In the discussion of all cases be sure to talk about damages. What if the grass and the flowers were not damaged? Bob Fingleprint tiptoed one or two steps. What damage did he do? Should he be punished? What if someone else saw? If Bob gets away with it, will it be fair to others?

4. After going through the test cases, review the qualities for a good law and rewrite the law to conform to your new standards. Let the students read aloud their reworded laws. Others should listen for holes or poor wording.

Extension activity:

Exchange laws. Have students write scenarios they think would test the other people's laws, showing that there is still a problem with them.

Have students go back and look at the laws they wrote in lesson 21 to see if they are just and fair.

Lesson 24

Objective: Students will be able to judge several cases using the laws of negligence and trespass and defend their decisions.

Accompanying Worksheet: Judgement of Modern Cases, pages 55-58

Procedure:

The five cases deal with laws of negligence or trespass. Students are to make judgements for each case. The review of the cases may be handled in two ways:

1. Read them out loud and follow with a group discussion, or

2. Act out each case with students taking the parts of lawyers, witnesses, jury and judge. This is by far the most successful way to develop understanding of cases resolved by judgement. If you choose to use this format, forms are included for student's courtroom presentations (pages 59-64).

3. You may want to discuss the fact that case 4, The Blocked Bridge, is a parallel to the 1990 incident that involved the Mohawks on the Canadian-U.S. border. In their efforts to force aboriginal land claims they blocked a bridge to Montreal — a bridge vital to commuters. You may wish to research this real case of trespass and civil disobedience and discuss the results of the incident.

Follow-up

There are many cases, either in texts or in the daily newspaper that can be dramatized in the classroom if you wish to have your class gain a more thorough knowledge of the workings of the law. A courtroom visit is also valuable.

Name_____

Three Types of Evaluation

People usually employ several different evaluation techniques before arriving at a decision. The technique that is used depends on the decision situation. There are three main techniques for evaluating situations and arriving at a decision. They are criteria evaluation, value judgement and judicial decision.

Criteria Evaluation

This type of evaluation is used when you come to a conclusion by assigning numbers that are based on some given criteria and then choosing the best by adding the ratings for each record, contestant or idea. This type of evaluation is used for things like report cards, figure skating, gymnastics and diving. Usually several marks are averaged to get a final score. Someone (a teacher or an expert judge) awards points or numbers. The judges have qualities they are looking for when they award the marks. These qualities are the criteria used to evaluate the work.

Value Judgement

In this type of evaluation your emotions and values are involved. What you feel intuitively is important. Usually the outcome, your decision, is based upon past experience as well as upon the circumstances at hand. Your moral training at home, at school and at church underlies the choice you make. Often these decisions are difficult to make because there is no right choice, and not to decide is, in fact, a decision. When these situations are difficult and deciding is hard, they are called dilemmas.

Judicial Decision

This type of evaluation is based on weighing the facts. Usually two or more groups have opposing opinions. Each side presents the facts as they see them. Rules or laws can be applied and past decisions for similar problems can influence the outcome. Usually there is a formal argument or debate before the conclusion is reached. This is how our law system works.

Name_____

Three Types of Evaluation, continued

For each situation, tell whether it is a situation that requires criteria evaluation, value judgement or judicial decision-making by putting a **CE, VJ,** or **JD** on the line in front of the description.

_____1. You have to decide whether to go to a friend's birthday party or a camping trip with your family.

_____2. You conduct a study to find out which store offers the cheapest prices and best service.

_____3. You are the judge in the Best of the Bunch Doggie Show.

_____4. You must decide who is at fault in a fight on the playground.

_____5. You are faced with a situation where you must decide whether to tell the truth and hurt someone's feelings or tell a small lie.

_____6. Someone broke a school rule. You have to listen to their side of the story and decide if they should be punished.

_____7. You have to decide whether to play baseball with your friends or study for a math test so you can get a good grade.

_____8. You are a judge for the local beauty pageant in which contestants are judged on beauty, poise and academic performance.

Write one example of a situation in which you would use each type of evaluation.

1. Criteria evaluation   _____

_____

2. Value judgement   _____

_____

3. Judicial decision   _____

_____

Name_____

Considering Criteria

When you make a decision you are considering several different factors. We call the factors **criteria**. You may just have one criterion. For instance, you may only be concerned with price when you decide which can of beans to buy. You may, however, have several things you want to consider before making a decision. For instance, if you're deciding which pair of jeans to buy, you may want to judge each pair in terms of style, fit, quality and price.

For each of the following situations choose the three criteria that would be most important to you in making a decision. Put a * by your three choices.

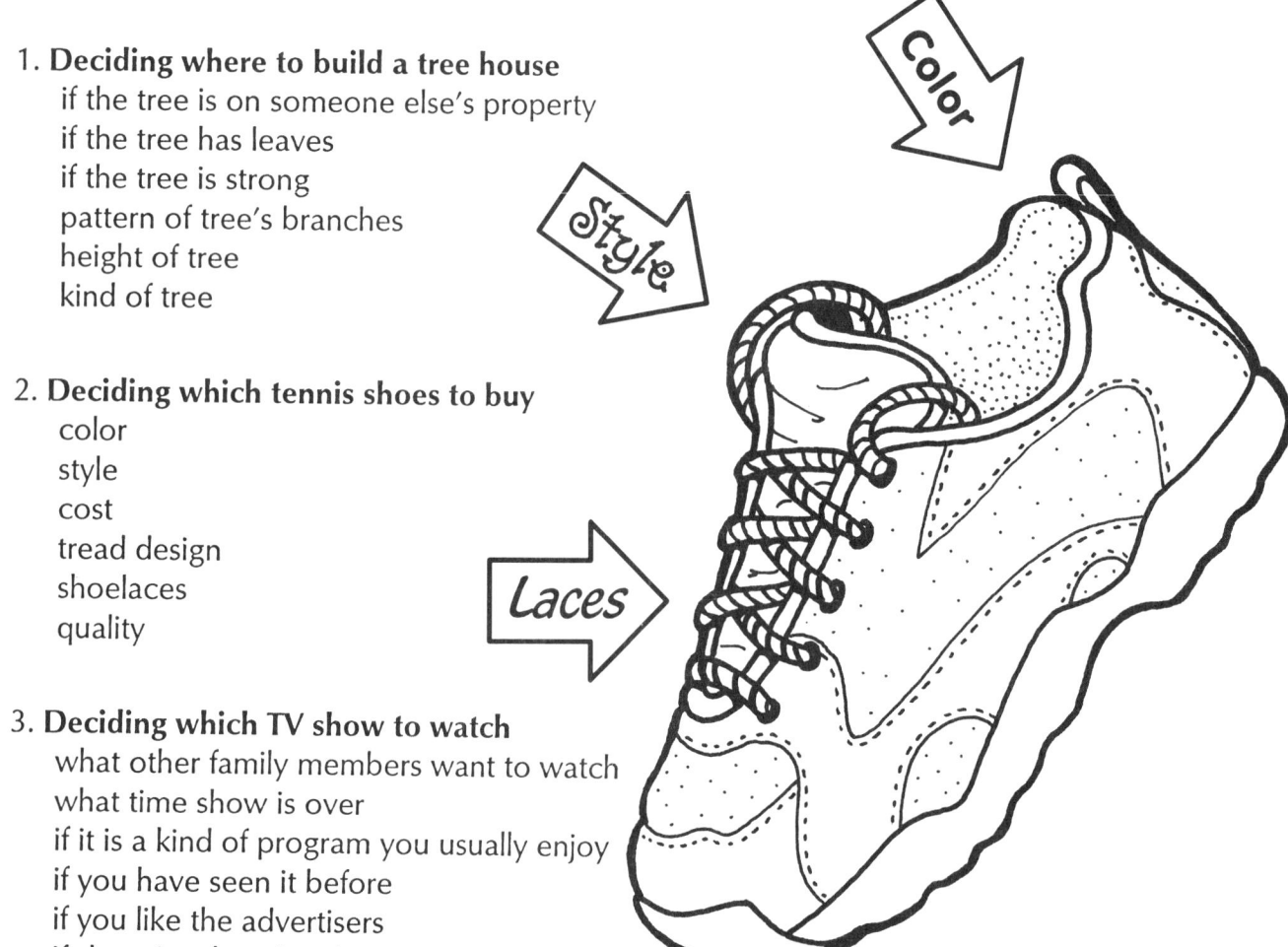

1. **Deciding where to build a tree house**
   if the tree is on someone else's property
   if the tree has leaves
   if the tree is strong
   pattern of tree's branches
   height of tree
   kind of tree

2. **Deciding which tennis shoes to buy**
   color
   style
   cost
   tread design
   shoelaces
   quality

3. **Deciding which TV show to watch**
   what other family members want to watch
   what time show is over
   if it is a kind of program you usually enjoy
   if you have seen it before
   if you like the advertisers
   if show is educational

4. **Choosing someone to receive the most valuable player award on the baseball team**
   how uniform looks on them
   how many points he/she has made during the season
   cooperation with rest of the team
   how much money his/her parents donated to the team
   sportsmanship
   catching skills

Name_____

Brainstorming Criteria

Money for a Concert

Read the following situation. Write as many ideas as possible. Continue on another piece of paper if you need more room.

A sensational new group is going to give a concert in your area. Your parents say you can go if you can earn the money for the tickets. You have two months before the group arrives. Think of all the ways you might earn the money.

_____   _____

_____   _____

_____   _____

_____   _____

_____   _____

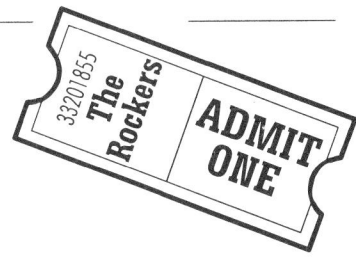

Use this evaluation chart to evaluate your ideas. Write your five best ideas on the chart. Use the criteria to rate each idea by assigning the numbers 1 to 5, with 5 being best or top rating. Each number may be used only once for each criterion. Total scores. Make your decision by choosing the idea with the highest score.

Criteria

1. Can you earn $30?

2. Will the work be hard or unpleasant?

3. Will your parents let you do it?

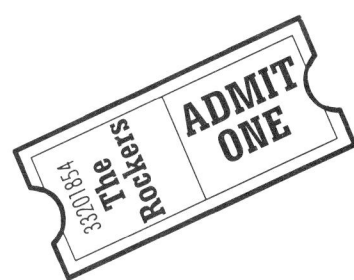

Best Ideas	criteria			
	1	2	3	Total
1.				
2.				
3.				
4.				
5.				

Name_____

Brainstorming Criteria

Class Party

Read the following situation. Write as many ideas as possible. Continue on another piece of paper if you need more room.

Your group has been chosen to plan the activities for the up-coming class party. Your task is to think up as many ideas for party activities as possible. Don't judge them now. Come up with as long a list as possible. Remember, a party's success or failure often hinges on fun activities.

_____   _____

_____   _____

_____   _____

_____   _____

Use this evaluation chart to evaluate your ideas. Write your five best ideas on the chart. Use the criteria to rate each idea by assigning the numbers 1 to 5, with 5 being best or top rating. Each number may be used only once for each criterion. Total scores. Make your decision by choosing the idea with the highest score.

Criteria

1. Will all or most of the students enjoy it and take part?
2. Will it be easy to organize and clean up?
3. Is it original and exciting without being goofy?

Best Ideas	criteria			
	1	2	3	Total
1.				
2.				
3.				
4.				
5.				

Name_____

Brainstorming Criteria

Math Center

Read the following situation. Write as many ideas as possible. Continue on another piece of paper if you need more room.

You have been asked to set up a math center in your classroom. This center is for students to work at when their other assignments are completed. What work or activities could you put at this center?

_____

_____

_____   _____

_____   _____

_____   _____

_____

Use this evaluation chart to evaluate your ideas. Write your five best ideas on the chart. Use the criteria to rate each idea by assigning the numbers 1 to 5, with 5 being best or top rating. Each number may be used only once for each criterion. Total scores. Make your decision by choosing the idea with the highest score.

Criteria

1. Is it educational?
2. Will students want to do it?
3. Can it be understood without a lot of explanation from the teacher?

Best Ideas	criteria			
	1	2	3	Total
1.				
2.				
3.				
4.				
5.				

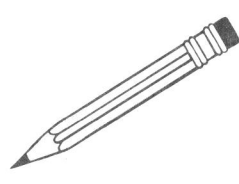

Name_____

Making Rules to Evaluate Your Ideas

People use rules or standards to judge things or for making choices. These rules are called criteria. Here is an example:

Linda Huppe has a choice of two schools to attend next year. Here some things she might think about (some criteria) before she makes her decision.

1. Which school her best friend is planning to attend
2. The distance from her home
3. The classes she can take
4. The extra curricular opportunities

For each of the following situations, list five or more criteria you might use in deciding what to do or which choice to make.

1. You've been asked to buy your teacher a year-end gift with money collected by the class. What criteria will you use when selecting the gift?

1. _____

2. _____

3. _____

4. _____

5. _____

Name_____

Making Rules to Evaluate Your Ideas, continued

2. You attended an expensive concert given by a nationally-known group. It didn't turn out to be great. What criteria did you use in deciding that it wasn't worth it?

   1. _____
   2. _____
   3. _____
   4. _____
   5. _____

3. You're planning a surprise party for your best friend. What criteria will you use when you plan the menu?

   1. _____
   2. _____
   3. _____
   4. _____
   5. _____

4. Bob White's entry was chosen as best in the conservation poster contest. What criteria do you think the judges used in judging the posters?

   1. _____

   _____

   2. _____

   _____

   3. _____
   4. _____
   5. _____

Name_____

Choosing a Class President

Criteria Selection

The students of Ryerson School plan to hold elections for president of the student council. Four people are campaigning for the position. Before you can make your selection for the best candidate, you will need to establish the criteria you will use to judge the candidates.

There are two parts to this activity. First, with a partner, list the personal qualities a good candidate must have. Then list the changes or improvements you would like to see made in order to make your school better.

Personal qualities

_____

_____

_____

_____

_____

_____

_____

_____

Plans to improve the school

_____

_____

_____

_____

_____

_____

_____

_____

With your partner, look at your lists of criteria. Choose the three most important criteria from your lists. Record these on the Candidate Evaluation on page 29.

Choosing a Class President

Candidate Description

Candidate 1 - Shirley Thompson

Background

Shirley has attended Ryerson School for three years. She's been active in sports and is the captain of the girls' volleyball team. Sometimes she argues with the referee when her side loses a point. Some people think she's bossy. She wears nice clothes and has the latest hair styles. Last month her older brother Tim got into trouble with the police for driving with a suspended licence. Shirley's grades are good. She usually averages a B, but during track season her math marks are a bit lower. She has a large group of friends and is friendly to everyone she meets.

Shirley's Speech

Hi. I'm Shirley Thompson and I want to be the next president of the student council. Ryerson School is a great school, and I'd like to show new students how friendly we are by forming a new student committee and by organizing new student get-togethers to help them get acquainted.

I'd also like to promote more sports in the school and buy equipment for sports we don't presently have, such as cricket and lacrosse. To buy the equipment I'd organize a committee to come up with ideas on how to get the money.

Last, I'd like to expand our after-school sports program so we can play more games in the season. This would help improve a team's performance, and we'd have a better chance of winning against other schools.

Last... I already said that didn't I. Well, this is really my last point. School should be a fun place. I think there should be a free play-day for half of a Friday every month. That way students could get to know each other better, and Ryerson School would really be a fun place to be.

Choosing a Class President
Candidate Description

Candidate 2 - Curtis Williams

Background

Curtis came to Ryerson School one year ago. He is quiet and studious and has worked as a junior librarian this year. Some people hardly know he's around and were surprised to learn that he planned to run for student council president. Curtis is tall and thin and wears glasses. He's an only child of older parents. His mother works in a library and his father teaches economics at the university. Curtis's marks are all A's. He's not involved in sports, but he does well during regular gym classes. He says his eyesight isn't good enough for him to be athletic.

Curtis's Speech

My name is Curtis Williams and I want to be your next student council president. The reason I want to be president is because I can see there is a need for more books in the library; especially the classics and books that would be good for research. Students at Ryerson who want to get into a good university must have good books and equipment to improve their studies.

I'd also like to start a student newspaper written by students about student events. This newspaper would highlight student accomplishments such as music festival winners, works of art done by students and special projects completed by students. There should also be special articles about students who achieve high academic marks in different subjects.

Some candidates make promises they can't keep. I think I can fulfill my promises to you. If you vote for me, I will work hard to make Ryerson a top educational institution.

Choosing a Class President
Candidate Description

Candidate 3 - Brent Hilargo

Background

Brent came to Ryerson School in the middle of last year from France where he lived most of his life. He had to be put back a grade because his English was not adequate. He has a thick accent, and some of the kids copy the way he talks and make fun of him. Brent doesn't seem to mind, and he takes the ribbing good-naturedly. Brent comes from a large family. To help out, he has a part-time job cleaning up his uncle's machine shop. Sometimes you can smell machine oil on his clothes and his fingernails have grease under them. His oldest sister won a scholarship and is in college. Brent's grades are generally good, although he does have some trouble with English.

Brent's Speech

Good day my friends. I am Brent Hilargo. I am hoping to become your student council president, because I think I can bring some improvements to the already excellent Ryerson School.

What I think would improve student-teacher relationships is more field trips. Students need to get out into the community more to learn about the world. They should visit small businesses in the area and learn what jobs are available to them when they graduate from high school, so they can plan their academic studies wisely. Students should have an opportunity to talk with doctors, lawyers, and shopkeepers to learn about economic and business practices.

I would also like to start a cycling club in Ryerson School. Where I come from there is the famous bicycle race, The Tour de France. Activities such as these build character and strength in students. Another thing I would like to institute at our school is a recycling center. We could recycle all our paper, aluminum and plastic. This would make our school cleaner and help the environment.

I would like to be an active member of this school. I hope you'll give me a chance by voting for me for president.

Choosing a Class President
Candidate Description

Candidate 4 - Colleen Moneypenny

Background

Colleen came to Ryerson School one year ago from a private school for girls. She plays tennis regularly and belongs to a private tennis club. She has joined the cheerleading squad and is active in drama. Some kids think Colleen is a bit stuck-up, but others say that is just her way. She wears designer clothes and throws a lot of parties. Her father has a senior position in the government. Colleen has one older sister who is married and lives in a different city. She has a close circle of friends of which she is definitely the leader.

Colleen's Speech

I'm Colleen Moneypenny. I'm running for student council president because I know I can improve the image of Ryerson School. With my connections I can bring a well-known director to Ryerson to help with the spring drama production. This director would be willing to work after school with people who want to improve in stage presentation, role playing and clear diction.

I'd also like to start a small orchestra for kids who enjoy classical music and are studying different instruments. I've had some training as an orchestra conductor. I'd also like to get more kids into tennis. Tennis is healthy and fun.

If you mark your ballot for Colleen Moneypenny, you will be making a vote for drama, music, and sports in Ryerson School.

Name_____

Choosing a Class President
Candidates Evaluations

Use this form to evaluate your choices for class president. Record your criteria for the three most important personal qualities and the three most important improvements for the school. Write just a key word for each criterion. Use the criteria to rate each candidate by assigning the numbers 1 to 4, with 4 being best. Use each number only once for each criterion. Total each candidate's score and make your decision by choosing the candidate with the highest score.

	criteria		total
	personal	school	
candidates			
1. Shirley Thompson			
2. Curtis Williams			
3. Brent Hilargo			
4. Colleen Moneypenny			

Name_____

Putting Your Criteria in Order

One way to select criteria is to list them, then to rate them in order of importance. Here are some of the qualities of a good friend. Number them in such a way that the quality you consider the most important is number 1, the next most important quality number 2, and so on. This doesn't mean that number 15 isn't important in a friend. It just means that you think other qualities are more important.

_____can keep a secret

_____will lend things to me when I need them

_____laughs at my jokes

_____is able to think of fun things to do

_____is a good student

_____is always on time

_____her/his parents like me

_____is good at sports

_____stays out of trouble

_____understands how I feel

_____listens when I talk

_____sides with me when I get in an argument with others

_____likes cats

_____has about the same amount of money to spend as I have

_____can be trusted

Now compare your criteria of a good friend with someone else in the group. Add three other qualities you both think are important.

1._____

2._____

3._____

Name_____

Play Time

Make a list of at least 12 things you most like to do in your leisure time.

____ _____   _____

____ _____   _____

____ _____   _____

____ _____   _____

____ _____   _____

____ _____   _____

Now go back and prioritize your list. Number 1 will be the activity you like the best, number 2 the next best, and so on.

Pretend that you want to choose something to do this afternoon. Select your five favorite things to do. Write them on the chart below. Use the following criteria to rate each activity. Put a * by the activity you will choose to do.

Criteria
1. Doesn't cost much
2. Can be done in 2 hours
3. Can be done alone
4. Is enjoyable

activity	criteria				total
	1	2	3	4	
1.					
2.					
3.					
4.					
5.					

Name_____

Wish List

If you are like most people, you probably have a lot of things you would like to buy if you had an unlimited amount of money. Make a list of some of the things you would like to buy.

_____   _____

_____   _____

_____   _____

_____   _____

Pretend your parents have told you that you can have $100.00 to spend on anything you wish. You want to be sure that you make a good decision, so you are going to be very thoughtful about this situation. What are the criteria you will use to help you decide what to buy?

1. cost $100.00 or less

2._____

3._____

4._____

Choose five things from your wish list. Use the criteria to help you evaluate each item. Put a * by the best item based on your evaluation.

wish list	criteria				total
	1	2	3	4	
1.					
2.					
3.					
4.					
5.					

Evaluating a Learning Experience

Now it is time to use what you have learned so far to evaluate some of your classes. Assume your principal is doing a study and wants to know what the best subjects are and why they are good. List five criteria of a good learning experience.

1. _____

2. _____

3. _____

4. _____

5. _____

Make a list of your classes. Use your criteria to evaluate each class.

classes	criteria					total
	1	2	3	4	5	

Based on your evaluation, which class is the best? Why? _____

_____

Name_____

Personal Preferences

Number the choices in each question 1, 2, or 3, with 1 being the answer you prefer most and 3 being the answer you prefer least.

1. What do you like to do most?

_____talk with a friend

_____play a video game

_____go to a party

2. Who upsets you most when you're working in a group?

_____someone who talks a lot

_____someone who won't listen to your ideas

_____someone who fools around

3. How do you prefer to be punished?

_____by being grounded for a week

_____by doing extra chores for a month

_____by taking away your spending money for two weeks

4. Which would you prefer?

_____to get a pet

_____to make a new friend

_____to go to bed a little later

5. Which would you like to do the least?

_____stay home alone overnight

_____change schools

_____move to a new city

6. Who would you like to be in your group?

_____just you and your best friend

_____4 or 5 friends

_____lots of kids

7. What's the worst experience?

_____reporting a friend to the teacher

_____being chosen last for a team

_____getting a poor report card

Name_____

Personal Preferences, continued

8. What do you consider the most difficult to do?

_____clean your room

_____write a story

_____make new friends

9. What kind of birthday party would you like?

_____a surprise party

_____a party you know about

_____a party you plan

10. What is hardest for you to do?

_____keep a secret

_____talk to the teacher alone

_____give an oral report in front of the class

11. Which of the following upsets you the most?

_____when your brothers or sisters get special privileges

_____when a friend won't listen to your side of an argument

_____when a teacher treats you without respect

12. Which is most important to you?

_____being popular

_____being smart

_____being athletic

13. Which bothers your conscience the most?

_____telling a lie to a parent

_____cheating on a test

_____telling a secret a friend told you

Something Extra

On the back of this paper give an example of how two people with different personal preferences would make different decisions.

Name_____

Decisions! Decisions!

Everyday events can produce situations in which you have to decide what is the right thing to do. If the following things happened to you, what would you decide to do? Circle the answer you think you would choose. Then give your reason.

1. The librarian should be told when a friend keeps a book and the friend says she lost it.

    yes   sometimes   no   not sure

    Reason _____

2. It's okay for your friends to vote against you when you run for class president.

    yes   sometimes   no   not sure

    Reason _____

3. If someone leaves a good pair of flippers at the beach, the person who finds them should make every effort to find the owner.

    yes   sometimes   no   not sure

    Reason _____

4. When you have a report on Ireland due on Monday and your team has a tournament on the weekend, it's all right to copy a report your brother did two years ago.

    yes   sometimes   no   not sure

    Reason _____

5. If a majority of the people are breaking a rule, it's okay if you break it too.

    yes   sometimes   no   not sure

    Reason _____

6. If a friend gets caught doing something wrong and you could help her by telling a small lie, you should do it.

    yes   sometimes   no   not sure

    Reason _____

7. When your mother tells you that your family has just inherited a lot of money and they want to keep it quiet for a while, it's okay to tell your best friend.

    yes   sometimes   no   not sure

    Reason _____

Name_____

Decision Situations

Often times we have to make decisions between two things, both of which seem important to us. In these cases, we need to decide which thing we value the most. This is often difficult to do, but the better we are at knowing what is truly important to us, the happier we will be with our decisions.

Read the following decision situations and decide which thing you would choose. Underline your choice. Be ready to explain why you made the choice you did.

1. You must decide whether to take a part-time job or try out for the football team. (money vs. fun and status)

2. A group of kids has dared you to steal something from the local store. You must decide if you want to take up the dare or not. (social acceptance vs. honesty)

3. You must decide whether to stay in at recess to finish your math paper or to take a lower grade and go out and play with your friends. (achievement vs. enjoyment and social acceptance)

4. You must decide whether you will go with your family for the weekend or stay with a friend and go to a slumber party. (family vs. friends)

5. You must decide if you will go along with your friends and do something you know your parents will disapprove of. (peer approval vs. parental approval)

6. You would like to join in the tug-of-war, but you don't want to get dirty. (enjoyment vs. appearance)

7. You must decide whether to give up art classes (which you really enjoy) in order to spend more time on your homework and get better grades in school. (enjoyment vs. achievement)

Name_____

Dilemma at the Birthday Party

"This is a great party, Scott," said his best friend Jon. The boys were taking a break from swimming while they waited for the food.

Mrs. Cornoyer, Scott's mother, came out to the deck. "Boys, I have to leave for a few minutes and pick up the pizzas. After you eat we'll play the last game, Big-Game Treasure Hunt. While I'm gone, I'm putting Gerald, Scott's older brother, in charge. You can watch the video I got for you. Under no circumstances is anyone to go into Scott's bedroom. That's where the special prizes are hidden." Mrs. Cornoyer picked up her wallet and keys. "Remember. No one is to go in Scott's room while I'm gone." Then Mrs. Cornoyer left to get the pizzas.

"Come on guys," Scott said as he put the video into the machine. "Let's watch this." The boys settled down in front of the television.

Gerald, Scott's brother, yawned then said, "While you boys watch the video, I'm going to make a phone call." He left them alone.

The video started and the boys watched for a few minutes. "I'm really excited about playing Big-Game Treasure Hunt," said Keith.

"Me, too," agreed Jon. "I've never played it before. I can hardly wait."

"I can hardly wait for the prizes," shouted Bobby. "Come on, Scott. Tell us what the prizes are."

"Why don't we take a quick peek," suggested Jon. He started walking toward Scott's bedroom. Some of the other boys followed.

"I don't think we should," said Scott. "The prizes are supposed to be a surprise."

"What will it hurt?" argued Keith. "We're going to see them in a little while anyway."

"I guess you're right," said Scott.

Slowly Bobby opened the door. "Wow! Look, there's all the prizes."

"Hey! What are you guys doing in Scott's room?" Gerald's face had an angry scowl on it. "You're not supposed to go in there."

Scott pulled the door shut. The boys looked ashamed and scared.

"Don't tell on us, Gerald," Scott begged. "We didn't hurt anything."

"Anyway, those prizes are for us," Keith said.

"You won't tell, will you Gerald?" Scott pleaded. "Mom might cancel the game. Then nobody will have a chance to win the prizes."

Suddenly there was a noise at the back door. "Hello. Where is everybody?" called Mrs. Cornoyer.

Should Gerald tell? Why?

Name_____

The Class Trip

Mr. Phillips dusted the chalk from his hands. "Those are all the details of the trip to Brown's Hobby Farm next week. First we'll see the animals, then we'll go horseback riding into the hills. We'll have a picnic lunch and go swimming in the creek in the afternoon. Any questions?"

The teacher pointed to the work on the board. "Okay. That's settled. Now, everyone down to work. I have to go out of the room for a few minutes to do some photocopying. I'm putting Marcela in charge. Everyone's to stay in their desks. If anyone makes any noise or gets out of his or her desk while I'm gone, we won't go on the trip to Brown's Hobby Farm. Does everyone understand?"

There were nods of understanding. Then Mr. Phillips left the room.

For a few minutes everyone worked silently. Then Everett leaned over to Carl and said, "I can hardly wait to go horseback riding."

"Me, too," Carl said out loud. He stood up in his seat and pretended to be galloping.

"That's not the way you hold the reins," said Aileen. "I've ridden before. Let me show you." She got out of her desk and pretended to ride up to Carl.

Pretty soon several people were talking and laughing about the trip. A few of them got out of their desks and practiced galloping around the room.

"Hey, you guys," Marcela said. She had to raise her voice to be heard. "Sit down. We're supposed to be working. Mr. Phillips will be back any minute. Then none of us will get to go to the farm. You're spoiling it for everyone."

"Someone be lookout at the door," Everett said.

David went to the door and peeked into the hall. "Here he comes." There was a mad scramble as several students dove back into their seats.

When Mr. Phillips walked into the room everyone was working. "Well, it looks like everyone is working." He put his papers on his desk. "Tell me, Marcela, did anyone get out of their seat while I was gone?"

Should Marcela tell Mr. Phillips the truth? Why?

Name_____

The Promise

Kirsten could hardly wait for school to end. Tonight she was going to sleep over at Diane's house. This would be the last time for a long while that she and Diane would see each other. They'd been best friends for years and now they had to part.

Diane's father had been transferred to another job in a new city. All week the family had been packing. The moving truck was coming Saturday morning for the furniture. After it was packed, they would be leaving for their new home.

"Come on, Diane," Kirsten urged her friend when class was over and school had finished for the week. "Let's go to my house and pick up my things. I've got the book of scary stories."

Diane was as excited as Kirsten. "My mom gave us permission to make chocolate fudge," she said. "And if we keep the sound down low, we can watch a video in the middle of the night!"

When the two of them walked into Kirsten's house, all was quiet. "Where is everybody?" Kirsten shouted.

They heard a noise in her parents' bedroom. Then her mother came out into the hall. Her eyes were very red and she was holding a tissue to her nose.

"Mom! What's wrong?" Kirsten ran to her mother.

Her mother hugged her. "We've had some bad news, Honey. Uncle William died this afternoon." Her mother started to weep.

"Oh, Mom. That's awful." Kirsten felt tears close behind her eyes. They stood like that for a few moments, then Kirsten stepped back. "I'll be home sometime tomorrow afternoon, Mom," Kirsten said.

"Kirsten, you can't go to Diane's tonight. Don't you understand? Your uncle died today."

"But, Mom. It's my last chance to be with Diane. After tomorrow I won't see her for at least a year. She's leaving tomorrow."

"No, Kirsten," her mother said.

"But, Mom, you promised!"

What do you think should happen? Should Kirsten be allowed to go to Diane's for a sleep-over, or should Kirsten have to stay home with her family? Why?

Name_____

The Garden

You and your friend have been lost on a desert island for many years. There is fresh water, fruit in the trees and fish in the streams for food. You get along very well. The two of you have built a comfortable shelter and you have fashioned furniture from island resources. Your friend is an avid gardener and has a beautiful garden that your friend works on every day. While your friend really enjoys the garden, you hate gardening.

Suddenly your friend becomes deathly ill. Your friend lies dying in your arms and asks you one last favor. Your friend asks you to promise to keep up the garden. You agree. Your friend dies.

1. Write down all the reasons you can think of why you should keep up the garden.

_____

_____

_____

2. Write down all the reasons you can think of why you shouldn't keep up the garden.

_____

_____

_____

3. Which choice will you make? Will you keep up the garden or let the garden die?

_____

4. Which of the reasons you gave above are most important to you?

_____

Share the Wealth

The year is 2020. Your father is a famous astronaut. For years he has explored the outer galaxies, and recently he discovered a wonderful new planet, very much like Earth but better.

Your family has been asked to be the first family to colonize this wonderful new place. You, your mother, and your two brothers are wildly excited. This new land promises to be a paradise. Unfortunately, you cannot take any of your earthly possessions with you, except for a few small personal items.

Your mother and father are intelligent, hard-working people and over the years they have amassed considerable wealth and property. Each member of the family has been asked to decide who will get the family possessions you cannot take with you.

This is what your family owns.

FAMILY POSSESSIONS

$100,000 in a savings account at the bank

A four bedroom, three bathroom house and contents worth $300,000

A summer home on the shores of Lake Silver Fish worth $90,000

An expensive sports car and a new van, valued at $70,000

A ski-boat with a 150 horsepower motor, valued at $15,000

Investments in stocks and bonds worth $200,000

Two pet cats, Tipps and Cool Cat (unfortunately there is no room for pets in the spaceship)

An old Rolls Royce your older brother had planned to restore some day, valued at $20,000

Your mother has part ownership in a small clothing store, valued at $50,000

A trunk full of old costumes, valued at $300

Your personal toys and a mountain bike, valued at $500

Art objects, valued at $10,000

Name_____

Share the Wealth, continued

First you must make a list of the people to whom you would like to give your possessions. You have family, friends and acquaintances in clubs and groups you are considering. Make a list of these people and tell why each is being considered.

Name   Reason this person is on the list

1. _____   _____

2. _____   _____

3. _____   _____

4. _____   _____

5. _____   _____

6. _____   _____

7. _____   _____

8 _____   _____

9. _____   _____

10. _____   _____

Now write your family will. Tell who will get each item.

_____

_____

_____

_____

_____

_____

_____

_____

Continue on the back of this paper if you need more room.

Name_____

The New Planet Dilemma

You are the leader of a new settlement on Planet Xnnos. You are light years away from Earth. Your space ship has developed mechanical difficulties and you and your group of 100 people are waiting for the space shuttle to bring spare parts. On the planet live 100,000 native Xnnosians. Up until now you and the natives have gotten along very well.

Suddenly one morning the chief of the natives asks to speak to you. He says that Smith, one of your people, killed his son last night. The chief wants you to put Smith outside the settlement limits tomorrow morning at sunrise so the natives can torture Smith to death to pay for his son's life. If you refuse to put Smith out, the natives will destroy your settlement and kill everyone. The chief of the natives leaves, and you can't contact him again.

You do some investigating after the chief leaves, and you find out that Smith couldn't possibly have killed the chief's son. Smith has been very ill in the hospital for the past three days and nights, and the doctor has been with him the entire time.

What are you going to do? Will you put Smith out even though he's innocent? Or will you have the whole settlement fight and risk (with great likelihood) that all 100 Earthlings will be killed? Remember, you cannot contact the chief again.

My course of action as leader of the settlement would be _____

_____

_____

The reasons for the decision are _____

_____

_____

Name_____

Breaking the Rules

"Let's do it!" whispered Danielle. "Nobody will ever know and it'll be fun."

Nine students huddled close together at the corner lunch table. All eyes were on Danielle. No one said anything.

Thomas tossed the remains of his lunch in the trash can. "I don't know, Danielle. We're not supposed to leave the school grounds at lunch break. We could get into trouble."

She addressed everyone at the table. "The trouble with you guys is that you're not willing to take any risks. Having to stay on school ground during school is a dumb rule. I don't agree with it. Besides, what can they do to us? We're a big group. Even if we're caught, so what? Come on. Are you with me?" Danielle looked at each of her buddies in turn.

When she came to Greg she stopped. "Well? I suppose you want to chicken out?"

Greg's face had a mottled look. "It's not that I don't want to. But if my dad finds out..."

The rest of the group remained silent.

"Okay. Let's plan it for Friday." Danielle put her hand out in the middle of the group. "It's a pact. We agree to absolute silence. No one else is to know. We're the top group in the school. Everyone else will want to know what's up. We're all sworn to secrecy."

Everyone in the group joined hands with Danielle until there was one giant fist in the middle.

"Secrecy," everyone answered in unison.

All week Danielle and her group made plans and by Friday they were ready. Leanne had scouted out the best place to sneak through the fence, and T.J. had timed the duty teacher's rounds. They had about fifteen minutes before anyone would notice that they were gone.

"Does everyone have money to buy snacks at the store?" Danielle asked at their last conference. "Okay. Anyone want out?"

"Not me," said T.J. "I'm ready to do it."

"Me, too. I'm in," came a chorus of answers.

They joined hands in the secrecy handshake.

"Okay. Let's go." Danielle led the way.

Would you have decided to join the group? Why?

Name_____

Judge the Situation

1 - Stray Cat

Actor 1. On your way home you found a bedraggled kitten being terrorized by a big dog. You saved the kitten, and because it was raining, you tucked it in your jacket and headed home. You will try to convince your mother that you should keep the kitten.

Actor 2. You are upset because your child has brought home a stray kitten. The animal looks sick and you cannot afford veterinary bills. You and your child had to move from your last apartment because your dog barked through the night, keeping the other tenants awake. You are not prepared to take on another animal.

2 - Stolen Video

Actor 1. You were shopping in a mall when a security guard came up and accused you of stealing. He says a person of your description was seen taking something from an electronics store and that you have it in the bag you are carrying. You do have a bag, and in it you have a video you bought a while ago then changed your mind and decided to return. You do not have a sales receipt for it.

Actor 2. You are a security guard at a shopping mall. You're sick and tired of kids who skip school and continually steal from the stores. One of the stores has given you a description of a young person who stole a video from its electronics department. You are determined to see this young offender gets what he or she deserves. This will deter other youngsters from stealing.

3 - Bad Grades

Actor 1. It's first term and you got a bad mark in language arts. You have to explain the grade to your parents. You've always been an A student and they expect you to bring home top marks. Because you've been a good student, you were asked to be on the student council and to work with underachieving students one day a week. You must convince your parents that one low mark is not the end of the world.

Actor 2. Your daughter has just brought home a low mark in language arts. You are furious. It is important that she keep her marks up if she is to go to a top secondary school. You think the best thing to do is to pull her from all extra curricular activities and curtail her social life until her grades improve.

Name_____

Judge the Situation

4 - Bed Time

Actor 1. Your parents went out for the evening and told you to be in bed by a certain time. You planned to, but at the last moment you started to watch a show that lasted longer than you expected. It went past your bedtime. Ten minutes before the show ends your parents show up. They are furious with you. You try to explain.

Actor 2. You had to come home early because your husband didn't feel well. You discover your daughter disobeyed you and isn't in bed. It's a half an hour past the bedtime you prescribed. You feel you must make a point of this or she may think she can get away with disobeying you in the future.

5 - Baby-sitter

Actor 1. You have a baby-sitting job at the Smith's. Little Terry is a dream to look after. However, the Smiths are strict about no company while they are out. Your best friend calls and says he has to see you. Your friend has just learned that his parents are about to separate. He needs someone to talk with and is afraid if you talk on the phone he might be overheard. You tell your friend to come over.

Actor 2. You went out for the evening and left a baby-sitter in charge of Terry. When you come home you find evidence that the sitter has had company while you were out. The sitter broke your strictest rule. You think the sitter should be paid less because he broke the rules.

6 - Late Assignments

Actor 1. You were supposed to hand in a research assignment this morning, and you planned to; but your cousin came for a visit for the weekend, and you couldn't do it. This was an assignment you liked, and you could have done a good job on it. You were late with your last two assignments, and your teacher warned you that this was your last chance to earn a good mark. You try to explain that it wasn't your fault this time.

Actor 2. This student has shown no responsibility to his homework assignments. He has received two warnings for past lateness. You think it is only fair to refuse to accept another late assignment. If you let him get away with this, he will not learn to be responsible and it will set a precedent for other students.

Name_____

Making Rules

You are part of a group that is about to colonize a new planet. Your task on this mission is to develop a set of rules that everyone must follow. What ten rules would you suggest for your new colony?

1. _____
2. _____
3. _____
4. _____
5. _____
6. _____
7. _____
8. _____
9. _____
10. _____

Now meet with another member of the group and compare your rules. Together choose the eight best rules.

1. _____
2. _____
3. _____
4. _____
5. _____
6. _____
7. _____
8. _____

Name_____

Making Rules, continued

The rules of a game may help the game run more smoothly or may avoid confusion or arguments. Rules at home and school and work usually relate to our jobs, our behavior or even the hours we do certain things. What do the rules you made tell about what you think is important? Do you think it is important to share? To protect property? To protect the young, the old and the weak? Go back to the eight rules and beside each write what that rule is concerned with. Use the following code. Add other codes if you need to.

Protection of People - PP

Fairness and Cooperation - FC

Protection of Property - PPr

Protection of Environment - PE

What are your main concerns about this new society on a new planet? Do the rules you made reflect your concerns? Explain.

_____

_____

_____

_____

What if someone on the new planet breaks the new rules? What will the punishments be?

Rule	Punishment		Rule	Punishment
1.	_____		5.	_____
2.	_____		6.	_____
3.	_____		7.	_____
4.	_____		8.	_____

Ancient Rules and Punishments

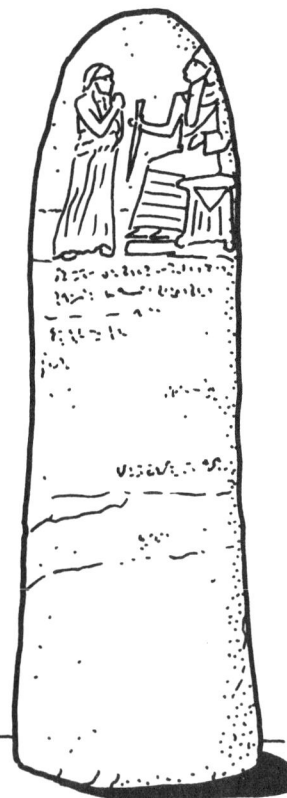

When people learned to domesticate animals and to grow crops for food, they were able to build permanent homes and settlements. This gave rise to a new problem, ownership of personal property. It became necessary to write down the rules and the punishments related to people's rights and to have the rules available so everyone knew what they were.

The first person to do this was Hammurabi, King of Babylon (1728-1686 B.C.). There were too many rules to remember, so Hammurabi had these rules and their punishments cut into a column of granite and had this huge stone placed in the center of the city where all the people could read it. Hammurabi's 300 laws dealt with matters of sale and purchase, inheritance, marriage, theft and manslaughter. Laws or rules made and enforced by a ruler are called edicts. Edicts made by the ruler or king generally favored the protection of the people of the ruling class and their property. The king judged all cases. His word was law.

The following are cases that might have been tried by King Hammurabi. Tell what you would do if you were the king. After you have made your judgements, your teacher will tell you what judgements were probable under Hammurabi's laws.

Case 1 - Errant Ox

Abdul was plowing his field with Bruno, an ox he had borrowed from his neighbor Thor. Suddenly a snake appeared in Bruno's path, frightening both man and beast. Bruno lashed out and kicked Abdul in the temple, killing him instantly. Thor, the owner of the ox, was charged with murder.

How would you judge this case? _____

_____

_____

Name _____

Ancient Rules and Punishments, continued

Case 2 - Stolen Payment

Hilgar owed his neighbor Babba money. One evening Hilgar came to Babba's house and offered Babba some furniture and a fine picture to settle the debt. Later it was discovered that the furniture and the picture had been stolen. Both Hilgar and Babba were charged with theft and receiving stolen property.

How would you judge this case? _____

_____

_____

Case 3 - Child Abuse

Kilgar's father had always been mean to Kilgar. Once when Kilgar had fallen off a horse and been hurt, his father called him stupid and cuffed him about the ears. And when Kilgar cried in his bed late at night, his father threw him out of the house and told him to sleep in the barn. After several years of this treatment from his father, Kilgar could take no more. One day when Kilgar's father picked up a stick to hit Kilgar, Kilgar struck his father. Kilgar was charged with hitting a father.

How would you judge this case? _____

_____

_____

Case 4 - Drunken Behavior

Poleth was visiting his friend Willim. The two men enjoyed an evening of drinking ale and telling stories. When Poleth was about to go home he was a bit intoxicated. He accidentally bumped into Willim's daughter, knocking her down the stairs. Unfortunately the girl hit her head on the cobblestones and died. Poleth was charged with killing another man's daughter.

How would you judge this case? _____

_____

_____

Name_____

Design-A-Law

As villages and towns grew, people saw the need to develop and improve the laws that governed them. They wanted laws that reflected a difference between deliberate and accidental acts, and they wanted to make sure that the guilty, not the innocent, were punished.

What are the qualities of a good law?

_____

_____

_____

_____

_____

Write a Law

Imagine that you are an elected official in Greenville, a town that prides itself on it's gardens, lawns, and especially on its beautiful Showpiece Park. You want to preserve your beautiful environment. You wish to make a law that will prohibit people from walking on the grass and picking the flowers in Showpiece Park.

Write a law for Greenville.

_____

_____

_____

What will the punishment be if someone breaks this law?

_____

_____

Name_____

Design-a-Law, continued

Test Your Law

Before your law passes final reading and is put into effect it must be tested to see if it covers every situation and deals with every situation fairly. Will it meet all needs? Does it treat people fairly? Will it punish the guilty and not the innocent? Examine your law with the following test cases. Read each case and tell how each case would be judged using your law.

Case 1. Mary Littlepink was coming home through the park late one night when she thought she heard footsteps behind her. Frightened, she took off at a run across the grass and through a flower bed of rare tropical flowers, breaking a number of them. Just then, the night guard appeared on his nightly rounds.

Has your law been broken? _____

Is your law fair in this case? Explain. _____

_____

_____

Case 2. Bob Fingleprint was an avid lepidopterist (collector of butterflies). He was walking through Showpiece Park when suddenly he spied a rare and lovely Funkweiler's Swallowtail. Bob whipped out his portable butterfly net and tiptoed across the grass to net the beauty. Just then the security guard appeared and arrested him.

Has your law been broken? _____

Is your law fair in this case? Explain. _____

_____

_____

Name_____

Design-a-Law, continued

Case 3. Linda Lookalive thought the new law was a stupid one. She didn't agree with it at all. Besides, she didn't vote for you when you ran for town council. In the evenings Linda liked to walk her German Shepherd, Poochie, through the park. Linda walked on the path, but Poochie roamed the grass. The guard caught them.

Has your law been broken? _____

Is your law fair in this case? Explain. _____

_____

_____

Case 4. Cathy and Angela met two cute guys at school. They decided to take the long way home through the park. The boys followed them. There was a lot of teasing and laughing. The boys started showing off and pushing each other around. Suddenly one boy pushed the other onto the grass. The guard caught them.

Has your law been broken? _____

Is your law fair in this case? Explain. _____

_____

_____

Rewrite Your Law

Think about your law in light of your general qualities for a good law and by how it worked in the test cases. If necessary, rewrite the law to make it better.

_____

_____

_____

Name_____

Judgement of Modern Cases

The Law of Negligence

Negligence is when a person does something carelessly and that carelessness causes injury to another person or to another person's property. A person will most likely be found guilty of negligence if that person should have known that injury or damage was likely to occur.

The Law of Trespass

If a person goes onto another person's property without the owner's permission, the person has broken the law of trespass. If a person is invited onto someone's property and then the person who issued the invitation changes his or her mind and asks the guest to leave and he or she doesn't, this is trespassing. The trespasser must be given a reasonable amount of time to leave. If the trespasser does not leave, the owner may use a reasonable amount of force to make the trespasser leave.

Case 1 - The Case of the Fast Ride

Mrs. and Mr. Jones' son Paul and his friend Jon were outside playing with Jon's skateboard when old Mrs. Williams, the next door neighbor, called the two boys over for a treat. Jon dropped his skateboard and the two boys ran over to Mrs. Williams' house.

Paul's father was an accountant who did his work at home. He was helping a client, Clinton Longclaw, fill out his income tax form. When the business was finished the two men continued to talk as Mr. Longclaw left. Neither of them noticed Paul's skateboard on the bottom step. Unfortunately, Mr. Longclaw stepped on the skateboard, shot down the walk and was badly injured. When he got out of the hospital, Mr. Longclaw sued Mr. Jones for his injuries and time off work.

Mr. Jones claimed he was not responsible for Mr. Longclaw's injuries. Besides, the skateboard belonged to Jon.

How would you judge this case? _____

_____

_____

_____

Name_____

Judgement of Modern Cases, continued

Case 2 - The Case of the Attempted Romance

Marjory Stellar worked in a grocery store. She had a crush on one of the stock boys, Bob Cornish. Bob tended to be a bit shy, so Marjory decided she would have to do something to make him notice her. Tuesday morning when Bob was carrying two large cases of tomato juice, Marjory tiptoed up behind him and surprised him. Bob swung around and dropped one of the cases. It landed on Marjory's foot, breaking it. Marjory was off work for two weeks, and during that time the store owner replaced her with someone he considered a better worker. Bob did not think what Marjory had done was funny, and he showed no interest in getting to know her any better.

Marjory sued Bob for damages and time off work. She claimed the accident was Bob's fault because he should have been using the two-wheeled truck to haul the cases instead of showing off his muscles by carrying the heavy load.

Bob insisted it wasn't his fault. She startled him.

How would you judge this case? _____

_____

_____

Case 3 - The Case of the Sticky Situation

Martha and Jane had been friends for years. Martha owned an old car and the two young women went everywhere together in it. Often the trunk lid stuck up in the air, and the two girls would laugh when they had to tug it down and slam it to lock it.

Finally Martha had the trunk lid fixed. That very day Martha was called away to her grandmother's funeral. Jane asked if she could borrow the car while Martha was gone. Jane used the car to go grocery shopping, and as usual when she put the groceries in the trunk, she tugged on the lid to close it. Unexpectedly the lid slammed down, catching Jane's hand and breaking her arm.

Jane sued Martha. Jane said Martha should have told her the trunk lid was fixed.

Martha said that she didn't have to tell everyone when she repaired her own property.

How would you judge this case? _____

_____

_____

Name_____

Judgement of Modern Cases, continued

Case 4 - The Case of the Blocked Bridge

Mr. Benjamin Troll lived in a small house in Deep Ravine. The Troll family had lived in Deep Ravine for several hundred years and the property had been handed down from father to son. In the past decade, though, the lands on either side of Deep Ravine had become populated by newcomers. Two large cities had developed on either side of Deep Ravine and a highway and bridge had been built by the cities to join them.

The rumble of traffic kept Benny Troll awake and angered him. The pollution from the cars was destroying the quality of air in Deep Ravine. Often people would stop and camp or picnic on his property. Wild flowers and animals were disappearing from Deep Ravine.

After one particularly bad weekend, when traffic had been jammed on the bridge for several hours, Benny Troll decided to put a stop to it. Late at night, when the highway cleared, Benny put up roadblocks and "No Trespassing" signs.

The next morning when people were on their way to work, they came upon the roadblock. Mr. William B. Goat was extremely annoyed. He was going to be late. With help from others, he moved the roadblock aside and tore down the sign. Traffic proceeded as it had before.

Benny Troll was furious. These people had no right to use his property. That night he built a larger earth and stone roadblock. He added barbed wire and painted two larger "No Trespassing" signs. Then he polished and oiled his rifle and waited for the trespassers.

The next morning when Mr. Goat saw the roadblock, he called for a bulldozer. But much to his surprise, before he could use the bulldozer to move even one stone, a warning shot rang out.

"Keep off my land, Billy Goat," shouted Benny Troll. "You are not welcome here, and I intend to protect what's mine."

After several attempts by Mr. Goat to cross the bridge and several rifle shots from Benny Troll, William Goat had to find another way to the other side of Deep Ravine. Instead of taking him a few minutes to get to work everyday, it now took him an hour and a half.

Mr. Goat sued Mr. Troll. Mr. Goat said Mr. Troll had no right to block a public road. He wanted damages for lost time at work, for the great inconvenience he'd been caused and for extra travel expenses. And he wanted damages for the car tires Mr. Troll shot out.

Mr. Troll maintained he had a right to protect his property from trespassers.

How would you judge this case? _____

_____

Name_____

Judgement of Modern Cases, continued

Case 5 - The Case of the Uninvited Guest

Late Saturday night, after attending a friend's wedding, Miss Beauty Locks was speeding home. Suddenly a deer leaped onto the road in front of her. Beauty swerved to miss the animal, and the car rolled down the embankment and landed up-side down next to Rushing River.

When Beauty came to, she was disoriented and her head hurt, but she managed to crawl out of the car. She had no idea where she was. On shaky legs she made her way along the edge of the river.

In a clearing in the middle of the forest lived Mr. and Mrs. B. Growler and their son, Teddy. The Growlers had chosen to leave civilization and live a much quieter life. They were not handsome nor worldly people and felt they didn't fit in with the fast-paced city life.

The Growlers usually awoke just before sunrise. Mrs. Growler would light the wood stove. While the porridge heated, the family would visit a wild strawberry patch a few kilometers deeper in the forest.

Shortly after sunrise, tired and hungry, Beauty stumbled into the clearing. She was relieved to see the small log cabin. She knocked. No answer. The door opened at her touch and she went in. The hot porridge smelled delicious. She helped herself to a bowl of it.

After she'd eaten she decided to look around. Surely someone was nearby. She looked in the living room. It was furnished with three rough chairs and a small homemade table. She sat down to wait. Before she could lean back and relax, the chair broke and she crashed to the floor. Horrified, she examined the damage.

It didn't seem that anyone was around to help, so she climbed into the loft. It was empty. Near tears, she flopped on the nearest bed, and in a few minutes she was asleep.

Suddenly she was awakened by loud voices. When she opened her eyes she was looking up into a big, angry face covered with bushy hair. Beauty screamed, leapt off the bed and raced downstairs and out of the house.

The Growlers sued Beauty Locks. Mr. Growler said Beauty had no right to eat his food and break his furniture. They were not wealthy people and could not afford this expense. The reason they moved out into the woods was to get away from people like Beauty Locks who thought she could do anything she wanted.

Beauty maintained the Growlers had scared her badly, and in her condition, she was lucky she found her way home. Besides, she said, if the Growlers didn't want uninvited guests they should have locked their doors.

How would you judge this case?_____

Name_____

Crime Report

Case of _____ versus _____

Detective(s) _____

_____

1. What crime was committed? _____

_____

2. Circumstances under which the crime was committed.

_____

_____

_____

3. Where is the scene of the crime? Give full address and a detailed description of the area and buildings. Attach a map if necessary

_____

_____

_____

4. People involved in the crime. Explain each person's involvement.

_____

_____

_____

_____

_____

Crime Report, continued

3. List the evidence you found (fingerprints, dead bodies, shell casings, bits of hair or torn cloth, etc.). Attach all evidence to this report.

1. _____

2. _____

3. _____

4. _____

5. _____

6. _____

7. _____

8. _____

4. List the names and addresses of all the people you interviewed. Give each person's connection either to the accused or to the victim. Attach copies of what they said when you interrogated them.

1. _____

2. _____

3. _____

4. _____

5. Whom do you feel is guilty of this crime? What evidence points to this person? Write a full report giving all the details.

_____

_____

_____

_____

_____

_____

The Case for the Prosecution
Pre-Trial Statement

This is to be read to the judge and jury.

The Prosecution is ready to present it's side in the case of _____

_____

We will try to prove that _____ (name of the accused) is guilty of

_____

_____

We have the following evidence:

1. _____

2. _____

3. _____

4. _____

We shall call upon the following witnesses:

Name   Reason this person is testifying

1. _____

2. _____

3. _____

4. _____

5. _____

The Prosecution will ask that _____ be found guilty of

_____

_____

Name_____

The Case for the Defense
Pre-Trial Statement

This is to be read to the judge and jury.

1. _____ (name of the accused) is not guilty of

   _____

   _____

   because _____

   _____

   _____

   _____

2. The burden of proof lies with the Prosecution. The jury must remember that a person is innocent until proven guilty.

3. We will show that the Prosecution does not have a case against my client.

4. We will show that the evidence the Prosecution will produce does not point to my client's guilt.

5. And we will present witnesses who will attest to the good character and the good actions of my client. In other words, ladies and gentlemen, we will raise doubts in your minds, and if you have the slightest doubt that my client is guilty, you must find him/her innocent.

Name_____

Cross-Examination Planning Sheet

Both prosecution and defense lawyers may use this to plan questions for their cross-examination of witnesses. While the other side presents its case, it is up to you to listen to each of the prosecution's witnesses and to prepare questions for cross-examination. Write them here:

Witness   Questions to ask under cross-examination

1. _____   _____

                                  _____

                                  _____

                                  _____

2. _____   _____

                                  _____

                                  _____

                                  _____

3. _____   _____

                                  _____

                                  _____

                                  _____

4. _____   _____

                                  _____

                                  _____

                                  _____

When it is your turn to present your side of the case, you may call your own witnesses and put the accused on the stand to speak for himself or herself.

Name _____

Final Summation Statement

Prosection - Defense (circle one)

This is to be read to the judge and jury at the conclusion of the trial.

> Your Honor, ladies and gentlemen of the jury, we have proved that
>
> _____ is (guilty or not guilty) of
>
> (crime) _____
>
> _____
>
> _____

If you are the prosecution write a short paragraph telling how the evidence and witnesses proved the accused guilty. Continue by reading this statement.

If you are the defense, write a short paragraph telling how the prosecution failed to prove beyond a shadow of a doubt that your client is guilty. Try to find fault with all the prosecution's evidence and with what the prosecution's witnesses said. Continue by reading this statement.

> _____
> _____
> _____
> _____
> _____
> _____
> _____
> _____
> _____
> _____
> _____
> _____